Volunteer U

Jim Angelakos
Christina Angelakos

Copyright © 2017 Angelakos

All rights reserved.

ISBN: 0692946470
ISBN-13: 978-0692946473

For Rebecca, Mia, Nicholas, and Rachel.

CONTENTS

	Acknowledgments	6
1	YOU, THE VOLUNTEER	7
2	SERVING WITH EXCELLENCE	17
3	FIRST IMPRESSIONS	31
4	CULTURE	41
5	DOING MINISTRY AS A TEAM	57
6	YOU, THE LEADER	69

ACKNOWLEDGMENTS

Special thanks to Sandra Tally, Wilfredo Vargas, Patrick Morley, Carl and Alice Stephens.

Chapter One

YOU, THE VOLUNTEER

Welcome to Volunteer U.

Ephesians 2:10 says, *"For we are His workmanship, created in Christ Jesus for good works, which God prepared beforehand that we should walk in them."* (NKJV).

As a volunteer, you might think your efforts don't really matter, or maybe you think all there is to your job is showing up and completing a task. Perhaps you've been serving a long time and love what you do, but feel you've reached the top and can't go any further in your volunteer role. Wherever you are in your volunteering journey, Volunteer U will help you recharge, refocus, find your first love, and reenergize.

You are handcrafted and designed by God to accomplish GREAT THINGS. It is our goal to help you become the best volunteer and serve with excellence, raising the bar for your organization and creating a new standard.

We pray this experience will not only broaden your knowledge, but it will also allow you to serve with excellence in all areas of your life: personally, professionally, and spiritually. May God richly bless your time here and prepare you to be His hands in serving and reaching your community.

Blessings,

Jim & Christine

VISION AND MISSION

"Where there is no vision, the people perish: but he that keepeth the law, happy is he."
Proverbs 29:18 (KJV)

Vision is  EXTREMELY IMPORTANT.

If we don't have a clear vision, it is challenging to do our jobs efficiently. How do we know where to go if there is no map? No blueprint for building? No plan of attack? Vision gives us purpose. It unites our efforts and allows us to achieve something bigger than we would ever be able to do on our own.

There is a difference between vision and mission. If vision is the overall goal of the organization, then mission is the strategy to accomplish this aim. Think of mission as the "by" or "how." For example, your vision might be, "To reach and disciple everyone in our city with the Gospel of Jesus Christ." How you accomplish that, or your mission, then might be, "By helping people Connect with God and other believers, Grow in their faith, and find ways to Serve God and people."

The vision is your what and the mission is your how.

You can never over communicate vision. Even if we've heard it 1,000 times, it's never enough. Our goal should be to continuously align our behaviors to match our organizational vision and mission.

Constant reminders of vision help us choose to do tasks that line up with our ultimate goal and avoid busywork that isn't faithful to mission.

⭐ Just because something is good doesn't mean it's right. It's okay for a heart surgeon to help take patient's blood pressure, but that isn't his role at the hospital. It would steal time away from what he has been trained to do. If a task doesn't ultimately aid in your vision and mission, don't spend a lot of time on it. God will honor your efforts when you focus on your vision.

At the same time, exemplary volunteers are constantly looking for ways to help accomplish organizational vision, even by performing tasks that don't automatically make sense as being on target. Phenomenal volunteers find work that connects to mission because they know even the smallest act can have significant consequences.

You might not think picking up a candy wrapper in the bushes outside the building is on mission, but think of guests' experience coming to the property for the first time. Believe it or not, seeing a well-kept parking lot really contributes to whether or not they'll even enter the building. Psychologists tell us that most people decide something in the first 15 seconds of their interaction.

Researchers call this "Thin-slicing" because it's the process of making a judgment with only a thin slice of information.[1] That doesn't give us a lot of time to make a good initial contact! But it's enough to cause a person to determine whether they plan on having a good or bad experience.

We'll talk more about first impressions later on, but for now just think about all the small tasks that contribute to helping your team accomplish their vision.

As volunteers, we need to:

- Keep our ultimate vision at the front of our minds while we serve.

- Choose to do tasks that benefit the organization, regardless of how important (or unimportant) we think those jobs might be.

- Avoid actions that don't support the overall vision.

My Church's Vision:

My Church's Mission:

There are four things you need to know.

1. You are Special

"I will praise You, for I am fearfully and wonderfully made; Marvelous are Your works, And that my soul knows very well."
Psalm 139:14 (NKJV)

There is no one quite like you. God has designed you with a unique set of gifts, talents, abilities, and even a personality that differentiates you from anyone else. Out of the 7 billion people on this planet, you were created singularly. Even if you found someone in the world that looked exactly like you, you would still be unique. Your characteristics, skills, likes, dislikes; they all combine to make up the exclusive one-of-a-kind individual that you are. When God's Word says, you are special...YOU ARE SPECIAL. There is no one like you, and there is no one who can do a task the way you can.

2. You are Loved

"This is real love—not that we loved God, but that he loved us and sent his Son as a sacrifice to take away our sins."
1 John 4:10 (NLT)

Only someone who truly loved you would have made you so complex and multifaceted. The Bible proves again and again God loves us and His love for us is much deeper than anything we've previously experienced. We see God lavishes His love on us (*1 John 3:1*). His love is steadfast and faithful (*Psalms 86:15*). The

Bible says He will quiet us by His love (*Zephaniah 3:17*), and in the most beautiful sacrifice known in human history, gave His only Son to die for us (*John 3:16*). And, not only are we loved, but the people with which we interact are loved just as much.

3. You have a Purpose
"'For I know the plans I have for you,' declares the Lord, 'plans to prosper you and not to harm you, plans to give you hope and a future.'"
Jeremiah 29:11 (NIV)

You were designed for a purpose. There is nothing accidental or unintentional about the way God created you. You have been intricately and lovingly crafted to accomplish a greater purpose. God has plans for you. Good plans. Plans that will give you a bright future. Never forget or devalue the incredible worth God has placed on you with the intent for you to live a victorious and fruitful life. The best is yet to come.

4. You are Needed
"For we are His workmanship, created in Christ Jesus for good works, which God prepared beforehand that we should walk in them."
Ephesians 2:10 (NKJV)

The world needs you. There is no one created like you, so there is no one who can accomplish things the way that you can. Your unique combination of skills, personality, and experiences are needed to make the world a better place. Don't buy into the lie somebody else will/should do it. YOU are somebody. Step into the role with confidence knowing you are making an impact.

You, The Volunteer
Discussion Questions:

Personal

- What are some of the things that make me special?

- When do I feel the most loved?

- What is my purpose?

    If you're not sure…think about what you are passionate about, what you enjoy doing, or what breaks your heart.

- Where am I needed?

    Keep your eyes open for areas where you can help.

- Do I believe that I am special, I am loved, I have a purpose, and that I am needed?

- If not, how can I start believing these truths?

Group

- How can we help others see they are special, loved, have a purpose, and are needed?

I:
- *Am Special*
- *Am Loved*
- *Have a Purpose*
- *Am Needed*

Chapter Two

Serving With Excellence
The Call To Go Above And Beyond Your Job

"And whatever you do, do it heartily, as to the Lord and not to men, knowing that from the Lord you will receive the reward of the inheritance; for you serve the Lord Christ."
Colossians 3:23-24 (NKJV)

THE CALL

Carl had an unusual hobby. He was jokingly known as the trash collector by the church staff. No gum wrapper, discarded receipt, rejected flyer, or soda can was safe when he was in the building.

Every piece of trash from his parking spot to the front door of the office got picked up and thrown away. On occasion he would wander some 20 feet out of his way, as he distractedly cleaned, moving from one forgotten item to the next.

Perhaps not so unusual, except Carl was the Lead Pastor at a megachurch.

Picking up trash wasn't in his job description. It wasn't something a guy of his position should have been doing. But it was in his nature. He saw something that needed to be done and went out of his way to fix it. Not only picking up items that were near him but going outside his radius to make sure the whole area looked good.

Convenient? No.

Convicting? Absolutely.

WHAT DOES IT MEAN TO SERVE WITH EXCELLENCE?

Serving with excellence is a pretty tall order. First off, what exactly is excellence? The dictionary defines it as, "the quality of being outstanding or extremely good." Okay. So we're looking to serve "extremely good." Grammatically that's terrible, but theologically it makes sense.

What does serving extremely good entail? What does it mean to serve with excellence?

The fourth chapter of Genesis gives the example of two brothers who presented offerings to the Lord.

These brothers had different gifts to offer God. Abel was a shepherd and kept flocks while Cain worked the soil. (*Genesis 4:2*). When it was time to bring an offering, both brothers gave from their personal inventory. Cain brought some of the fruits he had harvested (verse 3). While verse 4 tells us not only did Abel give a portion of his herd, but he gave the very best of all the sheep he raised. He offered God the firstborn of his flock. Both brothers sacrificed. But one stood above the other. Abel wasn't satisfied giving God a gift. He wanted to give his best gift.

Excellence is going beyond what is expected and offering what is extraordinary.

It is the act of raising the lid to people's expectations and surprising them with the unprecedented. *Matthew 5:41 says, "If anyone forces you to go one mile, go with them two miles."* People may expect one-mile service. It's bare minimum and normal. It's what everyone else does. What they are not expecting is the second mile. That's going above and beyond. It's uncomfortable. Inconvenient. Unexpected. And completely attention-getting.

Abel wasn't expected to bring the Lord the firstborn of his flock, but he did it anyway; and *"The Lord looked with favor on Abel and his offering..."* (verse 4). Abel brought his best and was rewarded with God's favor.

This is what it means to serve with excellence. Giving our best. Not just to the Lord, but to everyone with which we interact, everyone to which we talk, even when we're not thinking about it. Excellence should become second nature. Like breathing. It's something we do without putting conscious effort into it. It just comes naturally. We're always going above and beyond what is expected, and THAT becomes the standard when we serve.

DEVELOPING A LIFESTYLE OF EXCELLENCE

Excellence is a reflection of the God we serve. God created everything with excellence. As His creation, we want to be a reflection of that high standard. The problem with standards is they imply normalcy. Standards are not just a one-time occurrence or a single event. They are a trend that develops over time until it becomes a habit. It is consistency.

Excellence has to become a lifestyle. It doesn't just happen after one time. It is the cumulation of repeated acts until these behaviors become habitual. Whatever you do in life, whether you are working, playing, serving, studying, (Fill IN THE Blank), you must do it wholeheartedly. This forces us to live at a different level than everyone else around us. Giving our all is not easy. It requires focus. Discipline. Determination. Willpower. There's no easy way around it. Doing our best is hard work.

Consistency is key. We have to sacrifice comfort and current routines to create a new lifestyle of excellence. Then repeat, repeat, repeat.

EXCELLENCE VARIES BY DESIGN

Excellence levels vary by our design. We're fearfully and wonderfully made. The level of excellence that I have for something is not the same as someone else. Don't compare yourself. We are all different.

Back to our example of Cain and Abel. Each brother specialized in a different area. Cain was a man of the soil. He worked the farm, raised fruits and vegetables. Abel was a shepherd. He took care of flocks. Two entirely different gifts to present to the Lord, but God wasn't looking at what they brought. He was paying attention to how they brought it. Sometimes we're tempted to compare fruits and vegetables with sheep. That wasn't the point. The difference was that Abel brought the best of what he had, while Cain brought the leftovers.

It's all about bringing YOUR best to the table.

You can't be expected to sing a song with excellence if you're tone deaf. You will never be able to teach a class with excellence if you don't study the material. You shouldn't think you'll be the best nursery worker if you don't like children. We all have our own gifts and abilities. We can't equate what someone else is doing, with what is the norm.

Don't judge others. Don't compare. Don't be critical of yourself.

Our competitive world often makes us hyper-aware of others and how we measure up to everyone else. We constantly weigh ourselves against our peers to see how we stack up. Am I better or worse than them? Are they more successful or am I?

But serving with excellence is extremely personal.

There isn't a standard we can judge ourselves against. Excellence is, simply put, thoughtfulness combined with our best effort. Don't get distracted and discouraged with what others are doing. Instead, focus on how you can serve the Lord going above and beyond what is expected of you. Serve with YOUR excellence.

IT'S ALL IN THE DETAILS

Anyone can be a good volunteer, but excellence shows up in the details.

In London stands the beautiful Westminster Abbey. The exquisite chapel has been made famous by the coronations, royal weddings, and as the burial site of some of England's most notable citizens. One of Westminster's most impressive artistic elements is the detailed statues of saints and martyrs. During the renovation process, special attention was given to the carved figures which over the years had been covered in filth from pollution, pigeons, and age. The conservation team took the statues off of their pedestals, some of which hadn't been cleaned in over 300 years. To the shock of the restoration team, they discovered something extraordinary. The people who had sculpted the statues had spent just as much time making the back as they had the front. The details were incredible. Individual strands of hair, a complex fabric wrinkle, things that would be considered exquisite in the front but were astonishing to find on the backs where no one was expected ever to see them. What had possessed the sculptors to put that much effort in something no one would appreciate? A dedication to excellence.

Are we doing the same thing? Are we putting forth that much effort into small details no one will ever notice? At home? Work? School? Excellence is all about giving God the first and best of everything, as we learned with Cain and Abel. Even in places only we see. It is a dedication to the work itself, not the praise we receive from that work. Eventually, our efforts will begin to speak for itself. *Proverbs 22:29* says, *"Do you see someone skilled in their work? They will serve before kings; they will not serve before officials of low rank."* When you are skilled in your work, do your best, and serve with excellence, you will eventually gain a reputation which will propel you to the front.

Mediocre work and average work are not the stories we share over and over again in our organizations. It's the examples of people going above and beyond the call of duty which inspire us.

- The mechanic who found a part at a better price for the single mom who couldn't afford his regular items even though it cost him time.

- The waiter who overheard customers saying they were having a bad day and brought them a free dessert.

- The teacher who wrote the Afghan student a note in Pashto to encourage him when he did well on a test.

These are examples of unexpected excellence in small details. Excellence that earns people a reputation and creates a deeper connection.

It's not easy to pay attention to the small things. But don't believe the lie which says you aren't a "detail person." Everyone can be a detail person with enough concentration.

Here are some easy starters to help you become more excellent in the details.

- Stay an extra 5 minutes at work to complete a project.

- Write notes to remember things people say they like (or dislike).

- Get off your phone. It's surprising some things you'll catch when you're intentional about looking for them.

Work hard as unto the Lord. Your effort is not wasted. The Lord is watching and will give you favor in everything you do; you just have to put in the work.

Think about it like calibrating a compass. The magnetic needle points to magnetic north, not necessarily true north (the North Pole). Because of this discrepancy, searchers know they will need to make adjustments and rotate the compass dial until it is lined up with the magnetic north indicator. Small modifications are necessary to find the way to their destination.

We want to always excel. Just like resetting the compass. The Lord will keep adjusting you. Pivoting us in the right direction until we're headed the right way. Each day we get better. A little more compassionate. A bit more patient. Inch by inch, we keep realigning ourselves to head in His direction.

WHY DO WE CHASE EXCELLENCE?

There are a lot of different motivations for serving. What are some of the biggest reasons people serve with excellence?

Love.
Love God, love others.
Matthew 22:37-39

Gratitude.
Happy and thankful to be alive and serving.
1 Timothy 1:12

Eternal Significance.
Preparing for heaven and knowing the impact you have on others is eternal.
Hebrews 1:14, Hebrews 3:14, Hebrews 4:1,9

Rewards.
Rewards in heaven and this life. God blesses us and honors us when we do things for Him.
Mark 10:28-31, Matthew 16:27

Duty.
God has called us to do it, and so we have a responsibility.
Mark 1:38

Reverence.
Honor, respect, revere. We revere the Lord and Honor those that we serve.
Acts 10:2

There are also negative motivators.

Fear.
For example, afraid you'll lose your job if you don't do things a certain way

Insecurity.
Spurred on by an anxiety of what people will think of you

Competition.
Wanting to be better than everyone else

Negative motivators are not what we want to rule us. We want to focus on positive motivators.

Motivations might be a combination of the reasons listed above, not just one. There isn't a right or wrong answer; it's simply important to be aware of why we are doing things so we can adjust our behaviors if we have the wrong motives or negative influences. It's also important to remember certain things will motivate you differently. We take all this into account when considering our motivation.

Serving With Excellence
Discussion Questions:

Personal

- What motivates me to serve?

- Am I doing it to honor God or others?

- What am I passionate about?

- What are some of my gifts?

- Are my motivations pure?

- Do my motives line up with the Word of God and meet the expectations of my church?

Group

- Are we motivating each other to serve with excellence?

- How can we support each other in our pursuit of excellence?

BIG IDEA:
IS EXCELLENCE MY STANDARD?

Chapter Three

First Impressions
Where Every Interaction Is You At Your Best

"But the fruit of the Spirit is love, joy, peace, longsuffering, kindness, goodness, faithfulness, gentleness, self-control. Against such there is no law."
Galatians 5:22-23 (NKJV)

AT YOUR BEST...EVEN AT YOUR WORST

Emily was having a bad day. Two of her volunteers didn't show up; she had a paper due in four hours that she hadn't even started yet; and she just spilled coffee on her white volunteer shirt.

She had strategically planned to be behind the scenes this Sunday but ended up having to work the front check-in station at the Kid's Ministry instead. Now she was tired, aggravated, and had just given a name badge and a high-five to her 35th kid.

That's when the Rodriguez family came onto the property for the first time. With five children under the age of 9 and one of them having special needs, they rushed in late and looked more than a little flustered.

Emily took a deep breath. Plastered on a huge smile and kicked back into gear. "Hey, guys! Welcome! We're so glad you're here! Is this your first time?"

The parents gave her a relieved smile in return and took a few steps in her direction. From there it was a whirlwind of getting kids to the right classroom, organizing diaper bags, handing out pick-up tags, and making sure everyone got to service on time.

It was one interaction in the middle of a day filled with hundreds of interactions. It was a habitual, routine, behavior. But it made all the difference to that family.

Several years later Mr. & Mrs. Rodriguez filmed a special testimony of how they started going to the church. They had been to 13 churches over the 7 months they had moved to their new city, but they never found the right spot for their family, especially Jack, their son with special needs. When the Rodriguez family walked into the church that day and Emily greeted them, they made the decision right then and there this would be their home church.

To Emily who was having a rough day, it was nothing. To the family looking for somewhere to belong it was everything.

One interaction. One decision to exhibit excellence. And a first impression that ended up creating a lifetime of memories.

ONLY ONE CHANCE FOR A FIRST IMPRESSION

First impressions are everything. People make speedy decisions about whether or not they like something. For example, it only takes 7 seconds for people to decide how they feel about you; and most of the time people will reach that conclusion before you even open your mouth to speak.[1] In fact, less than 7% of first impressions are based on words.[2] Body language accounts for 55% and your tone or how you say the words count for 38%.[3] That means a majority of how people feel about you is based on non-verbals and is decided in a very short time span.

That's pretty intimidating. Does that mean we have to be on all the time? What about authenticity and being real about our feelings?

Giving a great first impression doesn't mean we have to be on all the time or hide how we're truly feeling. It simply means we have learned to put aside our emotions and moods to make others feel valued and comfortable. Whether we're having a good day or bad, feeling great or not, we're thinking about the needs of others instead of focusing on ourselves.

It also means we need to take how we present ourselves very seriously. If people are basing their decision of us based on non-verbals, we need to be aware of what it is we're "saying" when we're not talking. Are we friendly, open, and approachable? Do we do a good job of representing our organization? Do we show the culture of the church in our demeanor?

Smiling is the easiest way to make people feel welcome. You never know how something as simple as a smile can positively affect someone else. When we're looking for ways to make a great first impression, just think of what you would like to see if you were a first-time guest.

KNOWN BY YOUR FRUIT

How can we make sure we are leaving a great first impression? Like excellence we want it to become a habit. Second nature. Something that comes naturally.

Fruit is the result of a planted seed. The seed gets planted in the soil, watered, and slowly starts to grow into a plant. When seeds grow, they eventually bear fruit. We can't expect to reap something we didn't plant. And we can't expect to demonstrate behaviors that we don't practice and into which we put effort.

In our serving, fruit represents outward, visible response. *Galatians 5:22-23* gives us a good list of characteristics on which we should be focusing as we grow in Christ. Every disciple should embrace this marvelous set of inward qualities. As you read through the verse, here are a couple of questions to ask as you evaluate yourself against them.

"But the fruit of the Spirit is love, joy, peace, longsuffering, kindness, goodness, faithfulness, gentleness, self-control. Against such there is no law."
Galatians 5:22-23 (NKJV)

1. LOVE: Is my serving motivated by love for God and love for people?

2. JOY: Do I exhibit an unshakable joy, regardless of circumstances?

3. PEACE: Do people see my inward peace and take courage?

4. LONGSUFFERING: Do I wait patiently for results and take comfort in God's love when I'm in the midst of a trial?

5. KINDNESS: Am I caring and understanding toward everyone I meet?

6. GOODNESS: Do I want the best for others and my church?

7. FAITHFULNESS: Have I kept my commitments to the mission?

8. GENTLENESS: Is my strength under control? Am I tender?

9. SELF-CONTROL: Am I disciplined to make progress toward my goals?

These are the characteristics of someone who has been intentional. The traits of someone who is purposely working at exhibiting behaviors that will leave a lasting positive impression. It's not the easy way, but it is what is expected of us as Christians. Living daily with the qualities described in *Galatians 5:22-23* is hard. It requires a continuous realignment of our mindset. Death to self. But alive in Christ. Never easy, but always worth it.

How can we practice dying to self and living to serve others?

THE RULE OF BE'S

Naturally, it's not easy; but there are a few things we can do to serve those around us better. We call these the rule of be's. Here are 15 rules to give the best first impression possible.

1. Be on time

2. Be yourself

3. Be a good listener

4. Be interruptible

5. Be presentable

6. Be happy (smile)

7. Be positive

8. Be courteous

9. Be attentive

10. Be considerate

11. Be helpful

12. Be nice

13. Be gracious

14. Be kind

15. Be humble

As we follow these rules, we'll become more and more approachable. We become more accessible. We begin to demonstrate higher levels of customer service.

First Impressions
Discussion Questions

Personal

- Am I making a good first impression?

- Do I leave a lasting impression?

- The rule of be's help take the focus off of ourselves and care for others. How can we be more mindful of how our actions impact those around us?

Group

- How can we practice our Be's together?

Chapter Four

Culture
What We Believe Reflected In Our Behaviors

"Therefore, brethren, stand fast and hold the traditions which you were taught, whether by word or our epistle."
2 Thessalonians 2:15 (NKJV)

CULTURAL SHOCK

Jeff was new to the church. He and his family had just moved to the city and connected right away. They loved the program for their children and the engaging youth group that met Thursday nights. Jeff was excited to jump in and start serving. At his old church, Jeff and his wife, Lisa, led a small group for couples that would meet at different restaurants downtown once a week.

After getting clearance to start from the Small Groups Pastor, Jeff and Lisa excitedly began promoting. People seemed interested, and word spread quickly about the group. To Jeff's disappointment, at their first meeting they only had one other couple show up. The next week was worse. No one came.

Jeff felt like everything he was doing was failing. He tried so hard to get the rest of the team on board, but even with people excited about it, it just wasn't working out. Jeff felt frustrated and was starting to get burned out. How could something good, that had been so successful at their old church fail so miserably here? The problem was, it was a great idea, but it just didn't fit the culture of the church. The new church focused on small groups that met at the leader's house over coffee and donuts. People didn't need to hire a babysitter or pay for dinner because they were meeting at a neighbor's home. Although it was a fun concept, most people at the church just couldn't afford it or couldn't get someone to watch their children. Jeff was like a fish swimming against a current. It was too strong for him to get where he wanted to go. Instead of following the flow and working with others to accomplish goals, he had been wasting his efforts.

We should always be open to new ways of doing things and improving. But not all good ideas are right for our church. There are certain things we do very well. Things that line up with the church's vision and mission. But there are other things that simply don't fit with our culture. Understanding the culture of the church, what works, what doesn't, and how to maximize our efforts is key to being a part of a strong (and united) Volunteer Team.

WHAT IS CULTURE?

The church is a building, but it is made up of people within the building. They have a distinct identity all their own with a history, heritage, and a story of who they are and where they've been. You can learn so much by observing the atmosphere of the church. How staff members interact with each other and attendees, what artifacts are displayed, the stories that are passed along, even the way work is done. This is how culture is created. Culture is our shared beliefs and values. It regularly teaches, shapes, and forms people who are within it and vice versa. There is a one-to-one correlation between the Bible, our belief, and our behavior. The way we behave is based on what we believe, and what we believe is based on the Bible.

Culture practically shouts at you every time you interact with an organization, so it's important that we make sure our culture matches for what we want our church to stand. The personality of the organization comes to the fore, and you can tell in a heartbeat what drives the team. Our culture should match our values, vision, and overall organizational "vibe." When there's a disconnect between our culture and values, it creates tension. Frequently, the church will take on the personality of its leadership, but if there is another strong presence, the culture can make a shift in direction. Culture reflects in the behaviors of leaders, volunteers, and staff members. It appears in the undiscussed rules and norms of how the organization operates and is noticeable to any visitor who walks through the front door of your building for the first time.

We must make a strong caveat here that <u>culture is NOT the gospel of Jesus</u>. Many churches make their traditions into a litmus test of spirituality. Essentially, they "add" to the gospel of Jesus. It's legalism, and it's one reason so many young people have left the church and so many baby boomers are "done" with the church. We should never put any stumbling block in front of people other than the cross.

THE ELEMENTS OF CULTURE

Symbols—This can be anything that stands for something else. For Christians a cross is a significant symbol of Christ's sacrifice. In an organization, a symbol could be a logo or other graphic representations of who we are.

Traditions—Traditions are behaviors, activities, and events which are a part of the history of the organization. These are events that occur on a regular basis and often carry sentimental value with them.

Language—Phrases can play a significant role in creating culture. Key terms, words, and acronyms that are familiar to the organization and known to all members. Repeated verbiage.

Norms—These are social behaviors that are accepted in the environment. We pick up on cultural cues of other members and use them as guidelines for our behavior to learn what is and is not acceptable.

Values—Values are a shared system of standards. They are what is esteemed, respected, and appreciated by members of the organization or group. Values are often subjects espoused from the pulpit on a regular basis. If you want to know what a church values, listen to the topics of the pastor's sermons. Once values are set they are non-negotiable.

Artifacts—Artifacts are physical representations of the culture. It could be something as simple as the first dollar the organization ever made framed on the wall, a plaque with the organization's motto, or an old Bible that has been in the lobby since the church's founding.

FACTORS UNIQUE TO MY CULTURE

Your church has a unique culture all its own. You've probably felt this at one time or another. Many feel the culture of a church as soon as they walk through the front doors. There are so many different contributing factors to a church's culture, but unspoken culture might just be the strongest.

Unspoken culture is those items that aren't preached from the pulpit or pushed in team meetings. It's the unspoken "rules" that everyone knows but aren't necessarily voiced. Things like the dress code. Is your church more formal or laid back? Are jeans okay on a Sunday morning or is everyone wearing a suit? Issues like organizational hierarchy. Who runs things? Who do you go to for help or to make a decision? Attitude and the "vibe" of the church tell us a lot about the culture. How do people behave? Are they outgoing, friendly, and fun? Are there cliques? Is there a feeling of celebration when you come in?

Each of these different factors plays a part in creating the mosaic that creates the personality of your church. It's important to know what our culture is so we can do ministry in a way that compliments it.

Take a few minutes and think about the different factors of culture for your church:

Values

Artifacts

Social Norms

Dress code

Language

Symbols

FACTORS UNIQUE TO THE CHRISTIAN CULTURE

Then there are attributes, core principles, which belong to all churches and the general body of Christ around the world. As followers of Christ, we are a part of a larger organization than our individual churches. We belong to a huge interconnecting family, spread across many languages, cultures, nations, backgrounds, and denominations. This family has a unique culture of its own that transcends denominations and unites us in our love for Jesus.

The factors of culture in the Christian heritage are called many different things, but we're going to refer to them as Spiritual Disciplines. These are the practices that promote spiritual health and growth in the life of a Christ follower. Spiritual Disciplines help us stay on track, keep us constantly connected to God, and encourage us to love others selflessly. Some Spiritual Disciplines are designed to be practiced every day, helping us stay rooted in God's love for us and empowered to live victoriously for Him. Others are intended to be added to our routine every so often to develop us further.

Spiritual Disciplines in the Culture of Faith

Prayer. Prayer is vital in the Christian walk. This is our opportunity to connect with God in a personal way. Prayer is a conversation. It involves both speaking and listening. Prayer should also include more than just asking God for things. It's our chance to tell God how much we love Him, how grateful we are, and ask for forgiveness.

"Be joyful in hope, patient in affliction, faithful in prayer."
***Romans 12:12** (NIV)*

Remember the ACTS acronym: Adoration, Confession, Thanksgiving, Supplication.

Prayer has to become a daily habit. A good way to stretch in your faith and challenge yourself is by adding 5% more time to your current prayer routine. If you already spend 10 minutes a day in prayer that's only an extra 30 seconds! Try pushing yourself to increase your prayer time by 5% once a week and see what happens.

Bible Study. Reading the Bible is another one of those spiritual disciplines that needs to be practiced daily for it to be most effective in your life.

"For the word of God is alive and active. Sharper than any double-edged sword, it penetrates even to dividing soul and spirit, joints and marrow; it judges the thoughts and attitudes of the heart."
Hebrews 4:12 (NIV)

TIP: Read the Word out loud.

"Consequently, faith comes from hearing the message, and the message is heard through the word about Christ."
Romans 10:17 (NIV)

The Bible says faith comes by hearing. As we hear the Word, our faith begins to rise, encouraged by the power of the message. The more time we spend in the Bible reading it in a structured and organized way, the more we get out of it.

Download a devotional, start a read-in-a-year plan, join a Bible study, do something that keeps you on a planned track to get the most out of your experience.

Accountability. Give someone you trust permission to speak into your life. Set up a weekly or daily time to ask tough questions.

"Yes, what joy for those whose record the Lord has cleared of guilt, whose lives are lived in complete honesty! When I refused to confess my sin, my body wasted away, and I groaned all day long."
Psalms 32:2-3 (NLT)

A big reason people dislike having an accountability partner is because they feel shame. But shame needs silence, isolation, and fear to thrive. When you have someone you trust that you can confess and with which you can be accountable, shame and guilt lose their power. Remember, accountability should only be man-to-man or woman-to-woman. Never with someone of the opposite sex, unless it's your spouse.

Stewardship. Giving God back a portion of what He's given us is an important spiritual discipline. We've already talked about Cain's and Abel's offerings and how one was accepted while the other was rejected. 10% belongs to the Lord and should be invested back in the local church.

"Bring the full tithe into the storehouse, that there may be food in my house. And thereby put me to the test, says the Lord of hosts, if I will not open the windows of heaven for you and pour down for you a blessing until there is no more need."
Malachi 3:10 (ESV)

Tithing shouldn't feel forced or compulsory. God wants us to do it out of our love for Him not because we feel guilted into it. We decide to give God our best. Our best treasure (money). Our best talent (gifts & abilities). Our best time.

"Each one must give as he has decided in his heart, not reluctantly or under compulsion, for God loves a cheerful giver."
2 Corinthians 9:7 (ESV)

Fasting. Fasting is a great way to help us get closer to God, hear His voice more clearly, and separate ourselves from things that are distracting us.

In the Bible we see many examples of fasting before a major decision was made, in a season of difficulties, or to show humility before God. Combined with prayer, fasting is commonly found in the Bible as a means to purify, ask for direction, or plea for favor. Daniel is perhaps most well-known for practicing this spiritual discipline, and his fasts were always accompanied by prayer (*Daniel 9:3*).

"So I turned to the Lord God and pleaded with him in prayer and petition, in fasting, and in sackcloth and ashes."
Daniel 9:3 (NIV)

Fasting is an opportunity for us to starve our flesh and feed our spirit. We chose to temporarily give something up to gain a deeper relationship with God. It is a difficult trade-off but one that is well worth the effort.

Start small. You don't need to jump head first into a 40-day full fast. Try giving up a meal and spending time in prayer or reading your Bible instead. This is one of those spiritual disciplines that will take some work.

Active Church Involvement. If you aren't volunteering regularly, step into a new position and help. Putting your gifts to use is a great way to practice stewardship. God has given each of us a variety of unique talents and passions. There are many ways to connect these parts of your personality with jobs at your church. If you aren't sure what the best fit for you would be, ask your pastor to help you get started.

But active church involvement is more than volunteering. When you come to church, don't just serve. You need to be spiritually fed as well. Come to meet the Lord. Don't miss out on being challenged, convicted, inspired, and encouraged. *Luke 10:38-42* tells the story of Mary and Martha. While Martha was doing important tasks that needed to get done, Mary sat listening at Jesus' feet. Although her work was needed, she was missing out on being fed spiritually. Jesus prompted her to stop and listen. Sometimes we need to be reminded that same lesson. The work will always be there. We can't grow in our walk with God if we don't take the time to slow down and listen to the Word for ourselves. Things will get done. Our priorities need to be in place.

Spiritual disciplines keep us connected to each other and God. You should not be doing personal ministry without habitually doing these things, or you will get burned out. Practice the art of self-care. Before we can pour out, we need to be filled up. And not just filled, we need to have a constant stream coming from the ultimate source so that we can continually pour into others.

CULTURE CREATES UNITY

We talked about serving with excellence and how it needs to become a daily habit. More importantly, serving with excellence should be a part of your church's culture and it starts with you.

Do you want a culture of integrity? Serve with high standards. Do you want a culture of selflessness? Give with abandon. Do you want a culture of high-performance? Always come prepared. You are the catalyst for cultural change. It just takes a small rudder to turn a ship. Be the thermostat in the room and set the tone for the rest of the team.

Before bringing change ask yourself, "Does this line up with God's Word, and does it line up with our culture? Will it fit and work for us?" If your answers are "Yes" then do a small test, and see how to apply it and integrate it into the church. Honoring our culture is a large responsibility. We have to guard the culture and protect what God's doing in our organization.

The goal is to be all working and moving in the same direction. If one or two people are off and fighting the culture, it disrupts the whole process. Culture creates unity. We need to work as a team under the church's leadership to be at our most effective. When we're all on the same page, nothing can stop us.

Culture
Discussion Questions

Personal

- As a volunteer am I fitting my ministry into the culture of the church, or am I fighting it?

- Do I understand my church's culture?

- Am I submitting to the culture of my church?

- Am I practicing the culture of faith?

Group

- Is culture reflected in our words and behaviors?

Go with the flow

Don't Fight the Current!

Chapter Five

Doing Ministry As A Team
We Are Stronger Together

"For as we have many members in one body, but all the members do not have the same function, so we, being many, are one body in Christ, and individually members of one another. Having then gifts differing according to the grace that is given to us, let us use them..."
Romans 12:4-6 (NKJV)

THE DREAM TEAM

Nick, Dimitri, and Alex came to the church every Wednesday afternoon to set up the gym. Their church had experienced massive growth in the last year, and their youth group could no longer fit in the meeting hall. So every Wednesday at 5:00 pm these three would start the long process of setting up 300 chairs.

The men had nothing in common. They came from different backgrounds. They held different jobs. One was married, the other two were single. They were different ethnicities. They were different ages. Had different levels of education. But they had one thing in common. They loved the church, and they loved serving.

After a few weeks of working together, the guys got to know each other. They joked around; they figured out the fastest way to unload and set up the chairs. They prayed for each other. Their little group took on a new level of cohesion.

Soon, they had their set up done so quickly they started doing extra jobs to fill the time. They helped construct the stage. Rigged lights. Organized the back storage closet. They had become an incredible force. What started out as three strangers moving chairs, turned into a high-performing operation.

Volunteers have to work as a team. The team might be as small as 2 people or as large as 2,000. Regardless of size, the same principles apply. We need to appreciate our different strengths, work together, and serve God.

MOTIVATIONAL GIFTS

"We have different gifts, according to the grace given to each of us. If your gift is prophesying, then prophesy in accordance with your faith; if it is serving, then serve; if it is teaching, then teach; if it is to encourage, then give encouragement; if it is giving, then give generously; if it is to lead, do it diligently; if it is to show mercy, do it cheerfully."
Romans 12:6-8 (NIV)

The gifts described in this passage of scripture are called motivational gifts. They are spiritual talents God has given each one of us for the development and growth of the church.

Motivational gifts fall into two categories: speaking gifts and doing gifts. Let's take a look at the different gifts a little more closely.

Speaking gifts—Speaking God's message.

Teacher

One who loves to research and communicate truth. These people like to read, study, and communicate the Word.

Perceiver (Also known as prophecy).
One who clearly perceives/understands the will of God. Perceivers tend to be sensitive to the Holy Spirit and "sense" things about people.

Exhorter

One who loves to encourage others to live a victorious life. These are very positive people. They are often described as upbeat, happy-go-lucky, and glass-half-full types. People like to be around them because they speak life.

Doing gifts—Gifts of the body for doing.

Administrator/Leader

One who loves to organize, lead, or direct. These people thrive in roles as a facilitator, leader, and doing behind the scenes work needed for a service. They are often multi-taskers and enjoy juggling several things at the same time.

Compassion Person

One who shows compassion, love, and care for those in need. Those with the gift of compassion are often described as sensitive. They are the first ones on the scene at a hospital or sick bed, and they can put themselves in someone else's shoes and genuinely feel empathy.

Giver/Contributor
One who loves to give time, talents, and treasure. Givers see everything they have as a gift from God and are eager to give back what they can. These generous people tend to see the big picture and understand how their input will make a difference.

Server
One who loves to serve others. Servers are those people who seem to be everywhere at once. They are the first to volunteer, the last to leave, and seem to get energized by helping. It doesn't matter what task you give them, servers are always eager and happy to help.

God made us all unique. Special. Fearfully and wonderfully made. He has created us to do certain things that only we can do.

All of us have God-given gifts. We can access them at specific seasons and times when they are most needed. You are wired to do one or two gifts especially well. But you might have a blend of these gifts. We all have a blend of these. God uses that mix for His purpose. Even if you aren't naturally a compassionate person, God will help you become compassionate in certain seasons. A person with a speaking gift may not be able to do what the doing gifted person can do. God raises up the right people at the right time. We are all part of a team.

We can't compare ourselves. We were never created to do certain things. And that's okay. We focus on our strengths and allow others to focus on their strengths as well.

What do you think your top two motivational gifts are? (If you are not sure of your gifts, there are several free 'motivational gifts tests' online).

1. _____

2. _____

TRAITS OF A HIGH-PERFORMANCE TEAM

There are 10 traits of high-performance teams.

1. Shared Vision and Mission. A shared vision and mission are non-negotiable. Where there is unity of vision and purpose, you will find a high-performance team. First, the entire team should know exactly what the vision of the organization is. Second, everything they do should support those goals.

2. Excellence. Another trait of high-performance teams is never being satisfied with current progress. High-performing teams are always trying to do things better. They are not happy with status quo. They are constantly trying to be better, no matter how good they are. Even if it's perfect, they're not happy. They can always do better. Think of the pit team in a race. These guys are experts at changing tires quickly. But are they satisfied with a really good time? No. No matter how fast they change the tires, they are always looking to be faster. They aren't distracted by the other pit teams around them, the only competition they see is themselves. The goal is to beat their own time. Every opportunity they get. It isn't enough to be the best; they want to top their last time. Excellence is a continuous process.

3. Accountability. The high-performing team knows the importance of accountability. Members of the team give each other permission to correct, encourage, and put each other back on track when they get distracted. Teams who focus on accountability also understand they are part of a larger picture and need to submit to the rest of the team. *Romans 13:1-7* encourages us to submit to those in authority because they are accountable to God for us. Even Jesus submitted to authority. *Luke 22:42* shows Jesus told God, *"Not my will, but your will be done."* Ultimately we have the same responsibility. It isn't about us, it's all about God's will. What does the Master want? Not our will but God's.

4. Commitment. Commitment should be seen as an obvious trait for any team, but this is not always the case. A lot of teams suffer because members are inconsistent in their service. Commitment is based on keeping your word. Once you sign up for something, you should be all in. That doesn't mean you can't take breaks or miss a day or two. It means when you need a break; you let your team know. You're committed, so you don't want to leave them in the lurch. You care about their success even when you aren't there. Commitment is all about persistence, perseverance, and patience. You keep at it no matter how you feel at that particular moment. You're all in, and whatever is needed for the good of the team, you're going to do it.

5. Unity. Unity goes beyond just agreeing on a shared vision or mission. It is the act of working together to accomplish all goals (even if it is a different ministry or department). Unity is working together. In one accord. Call it being like-minded. Or having synergy. At its heart, it is the process of different people coming together to move as one. When everything is moving together in the right direction, it produces a lot of energy, excitement, a lot of focus, and a lot of power. Major tasks can be accomplished with much less effort due to the synchronization. Picture a horse drawn carriage. With just one horse a lot can be accomplished. It can carry large loads or even several people without breaking a sweat. Now imagine adding two or three more horses. How much more can they tow and how much faster when they are all moving in unison toward their destination? When we are united under the vision of God, submitting to authority and working together, incredible things can happen. Even if the group is only two or three people, there is synergy, and there is a stronger pull.

6. Trust. For a team to perform at its highest potential, there has to be complete trust among team members. The group should feel they can let their guard down. They feel safe with each other. They rely on each other to accomplish goals. Everyone has team member's backs. If someone is having a rough day, the other team members will protect, help, and care for them. Teams must also trust in God. *Proverbs 3:5* says, *"Trust in the Lord with all your heart, and lean not on your own understanding."* Teams who trust in the Lord know they can't rely on their own strength but have learned to respond to the prompts of the Holy Spirit for direction.

7. Training. High-performance teams are always being trained. Whatever you can do to continue your knowledge, education, and experience are well worth the effort. Consistently improving is the sign of a strong team. Each member works to hone his skills, so he will be more beneficial to the group. High-performing teams understand there is always room to grow. Ask experts in a particular field if they don't need any more training. You will hear a resounding, "NO." There's always more to learn, more to experience, more to practice.

8. A Servant's Heart. High-performing teams are always serving others. They function so well together they can accomplish difficult tasks without straining their synergy. Because they are so efficient they are not only performing their jobs, they are looking for ways to serve those around them. Whether that is their fellow teammates, their leaders, their followers, or guests, they are eager to humble themselves and serve. From picking up trash to running an errand for a sick team member, no task is too small or too undignified. Serving is their pleasure. It's second nature. Team members simply care about the team. Not just about the success of the mission. They care about each other.

9. Productivity. Another trait of high-performing teams is that they are always producing something. There is an obvious output to everything to which they put their hands. If the team is assigned a task, it will get done. No questions asked. For a high performing team, when things are operating and functioning properly they are showing results. Leaders come to expect a certain level of service, and they are never disappointed.

10. Healthy Relationships. The final trait of high-performing teams is healthy relationships. There is cohesiveness between team members. There isn't drama or personal issues. There is harmony and a general sense of enjoyment being with each other. On the occasion when there is an issue, it is handled maturely and resolved quickly. Team members value each other, and the respect they have for the group is reflected in their relationships. These groups know they must first spend time with the Lord before they can pour into others. When you are right with God, you will be able to have healthy relationships with others.

This is real love not that we love God but that He loved us.

God's high-performance team is the church...that's us. With all the different motivational gifts, abilities, and passions of team members, we're equipped to function at an incredible level. When we come to serve, and we serve God's way (in love, submitting to the Lord) we're a high-performance team.

Doing Ministry As A Team
Discussion Questions

<u>Personal</u>

- What am I adding to the team?

    This week, focus on strengthening any of the characteristics of high-performance teams we discussed where you may be weak.

- Am I using my gifts to help my team members look strong?

<u>Group</u>

- How can our team work together to maximize our different strengths and make up for any weak areas?

Chapter Six

You, The Leader

"When he had washed their feet and put on his outer garments and resumed his place, he said to them, "Do you understand what I have done to you? You call me Teacher and Lord, and you are right, for so I am. If I then, your Lord and Teacher, have washed your feet, you also ought to wash one another's feet. For I have given you an example, that you also should do just as I have done to you. "
John 13:12-15 (ESV)

Jesus was the ultimate example of what it means to serve with excellence. Though He was God, He humbled himself and performed a task which was normally done by a servant. He bent on His knees to wash the dirt from His disciple's feet.

This quiet action screamed His leadership perspective louder than any words ever could.

When they resisted, He explained that He did it so they would follow His model. Jesus never asked his followers to do something He wouldn't do. He led by example.

Jesus served His followers with the utmost care. Although He did the job of a servant, He was a real leader. His position did not constrain His power. Even in a lowly role, He held the rapt attention of the room. Every eye was on Him. Washing the feet of His followers was unheard of in that culture. It was unprecedented. It was unnatural. It was the last thing anyone expected. And it was a move that completely changed the way we view leadership.

As a volunteer, you may not think of yourself as a leader. But your position doesn't dictate your influence.

The term leader is deceptive because from our history books and grammar school lessons we've been taught that a leader is a famous, important person who led a military or nation. But the truth is, if you are looking closely, you can find leaders all over an organization and many of them do not hold traditional leadership positions at all.

We all remember that one kid in class to which everyone would silently look before taking a group action. Have you ever been on a team at work that's asked to do something, and everyone looks at that one person to see if she's going to do it first? That's natural leadership. Leaders are influencers. They don't have to be the CEO of the organization to have sway in the direction and culture of the company. You can lead from any place in the hierarchy of the organization. And volunteers often have more say in leadership than they might imagine because of their vital role in the successful production of the service. Without ushers, greeters, worship teams, nursery workers, parking teams and administrative teams the church would look a lot different.

You have the ability to lead from any place in the organization. Don't get stuck in the idea that your leadership is dependent on a title. Your capacity to lead isn't attached to your level of authority in an organization. If you see a need for change and have the passion for helping move the organization in that direction, you can do a lot without formal authority.

Remember, you are special. You are loved. You have a purpose. You are needed.

Now, it is your turn to tell others how they are special. They are loved. They have a purpose. They are needed. It's your turn to disciple. Your turn to teach them to serve with excellence, show them how to make a good first impression, follow the culture, and do ministry as a team.

You are a volunteer; now it's time to learn to be a leader.

WORKS CITED

CHAPTER ONE: YOU, THE VOLUNTEER

1. Winerman, L. (2005). 'Thin slices' of life: Psychologists are finding that our first impressions of others can be remarkably accurate — but also can fail us. *Monitor on Psychology, 36*(3), 54. doi: http://www.apa.org/monitor/mar05/slices.aspx

CHAPTER THREE: FIRST IMPRESSIONS

1. Ramsey, L. (2004). How to Seal the Deal in Seven Seconds. http://www.jobbankusa.com/CareerArticles/Personal_Aspects/ca80304b.html

2. Mehrabian, Albert (1971). Silent Messages (1st ed.). Belmont, CA: Wadsworth

3. Ibid.

ENCOURAGEMENT. INSPIRATION. TRAINING

Get the resources, encouragement, inspiration, and training you need to equip your volunteer team to serve with excellence.

LEARN MORE: WWW.VOLUNTEERU.ORG

www.ingramcontent.com/pod-product-compliance
Lightning Source LLC
Chambersburg PA
CBHW061341040426
42444CB00011B/3034